Teaching and Training Techniques

Lighting the Way to Performance Excellence

Spence Rogers
Jim Ludington
Becky Graf

PEAK Learning Systems, Inc.
Evergreen, Colorado USA

Published by
Peak Learning Systems, Inc.
6784 S. Olympus Drive
Evergreen, CO 80439-5312
phone: (303) 679-9780
e-mail: peaklearn@aol.com
website: http://www.peaklearn.com

For information, please call or write: Peak Learning Systems, Inc., 6784 S. Olympus Drive, Evergreen, CO 80439-5312. Telephone: (303) 679-9780; Fax (303) 679-9781.

Cover Design by Julie Lewis, Lewis Design

ISBN 1-889852-33-3

Dedication

This book is dedicated first to our families who support us totally in all that we do for kids and teachers, second to the great teachers who have taught us, and third to the teachers with whom we work to make a difference in the lives of others.

Acknowledgments

Success in life comes to those who find outstanding mentors. We would like to acknowledge all the teachers and other mentors who have contributed to our growth. Unfortunately, there is no way we can mention all who have helped us along the way, so what follows is a list of exceptional people who stand out in our memories for their immediate impact on what we are now passing along to others in this resource.

Rich Allen, Helen Burz, Steve Cousins, Katie Dix, Jim Foster, Kathy Gardner, Margery Ginsberg, William Glasser, Shari Graham, Thomas Guskey, Heidi Hayes Jacobs, Eric Jensen, Laurie Kagan, Spencer Kagan, Patricia Kirby, Carl Knudsen, Gloria Lewis, Robert Marzano, Deborah Pickering, Jane E. Pollack, Mike Rogers, Roz Rogers, Thomas A. Rogers, Jim Smith, Roger Taylor, Sue Tomaszewski, Sue Wells-Welsh, Raymond Wlodkowski, Harry K. Wong

Table of Contents

Part One

Introduction

Three Critical Domains and Six Non-Negotiable Keys for Successful Instruction

Notes

Introduction

Since the beginning of time, there have been great teachers who love teaching and whose students find learning to be a pleasant and highly successful experience. Great teachers are like Olympic athletes and other award winning performers. They have an abundance of effective strategies and a magical way of making everything work smoothly. That magic is called technique.

Effective technique in almost any endeavor is what separates the stars from the rest. The purpose of this resource is to provide insight into the powerful techniques of star teachers and trainers and into the magical ways they use those techniques to succeed every time.

Context, Content, Process: Three Essential Design Domains

For our instruction to be successful with virtually all learners, context, content, and process must be effectively managed.

Context

Context refers to the physical and emotional environment for the learning. The physical context refers to lighting, colors, sounds, temperature, smells, and spacing. Emotional context has to do with the feelings or emotional impact that results from being in the learning environment.

Content

We use the word content to include the specific knowledge, skills, and understandings that we wish the learners to acquire. Content needs to be effectively managed in that it needs to be carefully determined in terms of specific, observable behaviors that can identify successful learning. In addition, the learning needs to be carefully task-analyzed from the perspectives of what it is, how it fits into varied and valued contexts, and how it can be best learned. And of course, the last step to managing the content is developing and using effective on-going and final assessment tools to guide instructional decisions until the desired learning standard has been met.

Process

Process includes the style, strategies, and techniques that are drawn upon to ensure that the learners meet the learning objectives. Process applies to what we do to manage both content and context.

Notes

Page 15

Notes

1. Style refers to who we are as people—the personality, stories, and experiences that we bring to our teaching and learning experience.

2. Strategies are the multi-step procedures we use to:

   - establish and maintain an effective context
   - design and deliver the content
   - ensure that the real learning objectives are met.

3. Technique is the lubricant that ensures our strategies work perfectly and accomplish their intended purposes. Instructors who have mastered effective techniques will have smooth running classrooms in which students learn with pleasure and ease.

If your students are excited to learn what you have to offer, you can teach short of perfection and get away with about anything. But, the less interested they are, or the angrier they are about having to be in involved, the more perfect your equipment, setup, strategies and technique will have to be. Don't take chances; plan for the worst and always survive as a winner.

Six Keys for Unlocking Intrinsic Motivation and Reaching Performance Excellence

Your students are either with you because they chose to be or because some force has placed them there. If they're with you voluntarily, then your challenge is to keep them, but if they have had no choice about being with you, your challenge is to win them over. Regardless, the Six Keys function as a decision screen for us in the planning and execution of instruction.

Safety

People have a need to feel and be safe from fear, physical harm, embarrassment, or loss of dignity.

In order to keep our students engaged, we need to be certain they believe that they are safe in our teaching situations. With some learners, this is not easy to do and takes time. But with excited learners, the only worry is unintentionally creating situations in which they begin to feel unsafe and, therefore, withdraw or attack.

One implication of this key is that students need to

be able to opt out of any activity that may result in a situation they perceive as unsafe.

Success

For sustained motivation, our learners need a sense of success. This needs to manifests itself through recognition for past and on-going accomplishments while simultaneously providing visible progress toward new and challenging objectives.

First and foremost, our students need to feel our respect and recognition for their previous successes and accomplishments. They need to know we value what they have done so far. For reluctant learners, this requires deliberate efforts on our part, but for the others, it just requires that we don't accidentally, or deliberately, do or say anything that could possibly lead to our students doubting their worth, skillfulness, knowledge, creativity, and/or accomplishments.

Second, throughout our teaching, our students need regular, convincing, and valued evidence of their *progress* toward reaching challenging goals, and finally, their *mastery* of them. In a classroom, this cannot be satisfied by moving from unit to unit with less than what the student considers mastery unless the student is only interested in "just getting through it." It is important for learners to see themselves continuously learning more and more at a level they consider to be worthy of pride.

Love and Belonging

Feelings of inclusion, respect, acceptance, and being cared about are vital to people. This key is critical in several ways.

For many people, when they are not supported, held accountable for standards, taught things deemed worthwhile, protected, and respected for their uniqueness, it is interpreted as the "teacher doesn't care enough." Tragically, too often this results in the learners withdrawing, losing interest, and behaving inappropriately.

From another perspective, it is critical that our instructional practices:

1. Absolutely prevent all put-downs and sarcasm;

2. Protect every learner from any situation in which a student could feel excluded or not respected;

3. Incorporate effective leadership for building and maintaining collaborative, mutually supportive and respecting behaviors on the part of everyone; and

4. Use varied and safe cooperative, class-building, and team-building

Notes

Page 17

Notes

structures to ensure mutual respect, support, and protection across the group.

Freedom and Independence

Choice, individuality, and freedom from what might be perceived as excessive control or manipulation is important to all people. Determine what is important for the students to learn, what constitutes convincing evidence that the desired learning has truly occurred, and what is critical in how they learn what is being taught. Then let everything else contain options.

When our instruction is effective and our techniques are good enough, our students will most likely do whatever we need to ask of them.

Fun and Enjoyment

When students consider our instruction fun, entertaining, or enjoyable, they are more likely to significantly exert themselves. But, there is more to it than that. As soon as they begin to become bored, afraid, or frustrated, they tend to "drop out of the flow" and lose interest.

Valued Purpose

If we want our learners to diligently apply themselves, we must create situations in which they consider their effort and sacrifices worthwhile. This can be done in one of several ways. We can

1. Teach that in which the students already have an intense interest;

2. Teach something that will, from our students' perspective, solve a problem that they believe they have and want solved;

3. Build and maintain strong enough relationships with our students for them to willingly work at learning what we are teaching – even if they don't see enough value in it to otherwise justify the time, energy, discomfort, or expenditure of resources.

The bottom line is that our students will work hard to learn what we are teaching if they see enough importance in either learning the content or in meeting the needs of others they value. For many of us, this means we are constantly trying to make certain we never threaten our students' other five keys to the extent that they decide that learning what we are teaching is no longer worth the sacrifice.

Notes

Notes

Part Two

How to
Plan for Success
with Your Learners

Notes

Understand Your Audience

Research your audience before planning for teaching your workshop or class. Make certain you know their needs, perspectives, interests, prides, and hot buttons. Determine what the different factions are within your audience, and make sure you understand each. This understanding is essential for successfully planning your instruction, avoiding problems, making decisions on your feet, and working your way out of any difficult situations that may arise.

Clarify Your Objectives from the Learners' Perspectives

Based on your thorough understanding of your students, determine how to frame, modify, and add to your objectives to ensure your audience will be open to your teaching. Stephen Covey states it so well, "Seek first to understand."

Make certain that your planning is done through your students' needs or perspectives.

- What problems and interests do they have?
- What are they proud of and what do they wish would go away forever?

- What past history will color their receptiveness?
- And, what can you bring that your students already perceive as valuable?

Lower Resistance Before Building Acceptance for What You are Teaching

Your students won't hear anything you have to offer until any resistance they have is eliminated. Make sure you understand the basis of any resistance and develop a well-researched plan for washing it away – NOT for pushing it away.

If there is any chance you will have students who will openly attempt to block, defy, or derail your efforts, do your homework. Know their issues.

Research practical strategies within your skill level for preventing inappropriate student behavior from ever surfacing, and just in case, find multiple strategies for addressing problems that can arise with resistant learners.

Notes

Notes

Equipment and Supplies

Ensure that *effective* equipment and supplies will be available. Don't leave your success to chance. Your success will be significantly impacted by the quality of your equipment and supplies.

Projectors

- Use projectors that are bright enough that the images can be easily seen without lowering lights or shutting shades. In addition, projectors should have multiple element lenses for clear images, and they should project a perfectly rectangular image aligned with the edges of your screen. Anything less than 4000 lumens will usually not be bright enough for groups of more than 10-20 people – this is relatively easy to do with overhead projectors, but prohibitively expensive in most cases with computer projection systems.
- Replace the projector bulbs when the image begins to dim or turn yellowish – don't wait for the bulb to burn out.
- Extra bulbs should be readily available during your instruction for a quick replacement if necessary.

- The projector should be in excellent repair and alignment so the image will be "square" on the screen.

Projection screens

- The size should be large enough for your images to be easily seen and interpreted from where any learner might sit.
- The screen should be raised high enough for the students in the back of your class—in most cases, this means it should be raised to its maximum height.
- Screens should be clean and bright—do NOT use the silver, lenticular screens.

Microphones and Speakers

When in doubt, use a microphone. Microphones allow us to use a natural voice effectively without strain and still be heard. Though many professional speakers and experienced teachers can carry a group of up to 50 fairly well without a microphone, effectively using a good microphone and sound system will almost always improve your results with a group of twenty-five or more. In fact, many schools are now providing microphones for classroom teachers.

Tips for increasing your effectiveness with microphones:

1. Don't save money here. Make sure that whatever equipment you are going to use will produce excellent sound at any volume level you might need.

2. Windscreens are important – use them. They prevent popping and other distracting, unpleasant sounds from our breath hitting the microphone.

3. Always check the sound levels of your microphone system from throughout the room before you begin teaching.

4. Practice, practice, practice – there isn't anything much worse than struggling to hear someone or having to listen to the pops and other annoying sounds generated by someone using a microphone incorrectly.

5. Pick the microphone that's best for you.

- Headset microphones will produce the best sound in addition to working best when your head turns from side to side.
- Handheld microphones are excellent for sound also but require significant practice to ensure their effectiveness.
- Lavaliere microphones are nice for their convenience but tend to produce the poorest quality sound.
- Wireless microphones provide tremendous freedom for interacting among our students.
- UHF systems are better than VHF in that they are less likely to have problems with interference from other signals.

Notes

Notes

Music System

Music can be an incredibly powerful tool, but only if it is used well with effective equipment.

Players

Use a CD or MP3 player. These allow for rapid, random access to the music selections that you need exactly when you need them. Make sure the system is easy to use with very little attention, skill, or time. Downtime created by fumbling to make a system work, getting it started, adjusting the volume, or finding a selection is deadly – the learners lose interest and we start to lose control of the management of the instruction. Remember, nature abhors a vacuum – all vacuums will be filled if there is anything available to fill them.

Whatever the type of system you decide to use, make sure it has a *wireless remote* control. This will allow you to work your music quickly and easily from virtually anywhere in the room while maintaining good eye contact with your students. If using a CD player, those without changers tend to be fastest. We recommend single CD players. There are several good options available.

1. We greatly prefer using the Panasonic SL-SX392C portable,

personal CD players. These players have several distinct advantages.

- They come with a wireless remote.
- They are relatively inexpensive – about $65.00 each.
- They can be connected through the headphone plug with a set of amplified speakers – any set with between 10 and 100 watts of power will work in most classroom situations – this gives us great flexibility with the quality and quantity of sound we wish and may need. For working in situations that may require a microphone, these players can be wired into what are called monitor speakers, which often have additional inputs for microphones and/or additional CD players.
- They operate with easily changed batteries and without additional wire for electricity, which can add to the confusion and clutter in your work area.
- They can be wired into large sound systems through the headphone jack to work in literally any situation.
- They can be wired together with either a mixer or, more simply, a switch box from Radio Shack to

allow more than one player to be used at a time for tremendous speed and flexibility in a teaching situation.

2. Bose makes two excellent, though expensive, systems that will work very well for groups up to about 100.

Helpful Hint: Learn to use your system before you need it in a teaching situation. Practice extensively until its operation is automatic for you and you no longer need to look at the remote to use it.

Miscellaneous

-   At least one table large enough to spread out your instructional supplies is a must.
-   Breath mints and a mouth-refreshing, thirst-quenching beverage placed in your work area to keep yourself ready to interact with students one-on-one.

Plan for Appropriate Visuals

Use visuals to support your message – not to "out do" you or your message. Avoid a lot of flash, bells, and whistles – just focus on simple visuals that enhance your message and are easily seen and interpreted.

Whatever approach you use, check your visuals from everywhere your students might be. Sit and stand in every possible place, put your hand up in front of your face at arm's length to represent the height of other students' heads, and determine what you need to do to ensure clear visibility for all students.

Helpful Hints:

-   When preparing slides and transparencies, use light letters on dark backgrounds or dark letters on clear or light backgrounds.
-   Clean, new write-on transparencies are essential if you are writing on the overhead. Permanent, fine-tipped overhead transparency pens are best – Sharpie is an excellent brand.
-   Avoid fire colors (red, orange, yellow). They are hard to read and tend to raise stress.
-   Strive to stick with the 4x4 rule – strive to limit yourself to 4 lines of text with no more than 4 words per line. If you must exceed the 4x4 rule, NEVER go beyond 6x6. If necessary spread your text over multiple "slides" to maintain excellent visibility. Remember, your visuals are to enhance or abbreviate your message – not to be your message.

Notes

Page 27

Notes

- Plan on pausing as each projected image appears to provide time for your students to become familiar with it. If this is not done, many of your students will be ignoring what you are saying as they study your images anyway.
- Avoid using more than the top half at best or top two-thirds at worst of any image to be projected – your learners sitting behind other students will not be able to see anything at the bottom of your images.
- Check all PowerPoint slides and transparencies by printing them on 8.5x11 paper, putting them on the wall, and making certain a typical person can easily see and interpret them while standing at least 10 feet away. If the graphics and text cannot be seen and interpreted easily from this distance, the images and point sizes are too small and must be enlarged for a successful lesson or presentation.

Remember – if students can't easily see and interpret your visuals, you are not only failing to use one of your most possible available tools, your students will start to become frustrated, angry, and withdrawn.

PowerPoint

Presentation software can be a powerful tool for displaying information. However, use caution with PowerPoint and other computer controlled visuals. The projectors typically require dimmed lighting, and the templates are not typically designed well for successful presentations – especially with less than receptive audiences. When using electronic presentation software, exercise extreme care to utilize the best research regarding design, timing, and projection equipment.

Overhead Projectors and Transparencies

The technology is old, but overhead projectors and transparencies are still one of the best available due to the brightness and clarity of good projectors and the versatility with design and flexibility inherent in the approach.

However, just as with PowerPoint, take extreme care to produce overhead transparencies that can be easily read and interpreted from anywhere in the room. (See the section *Plan for Appropriate Visuals.*)

Flipcharts

Flipcharts are effective with small groups – *maybe* as many as a dozen people, but this would be severely pushing the limits of the medium.

- Make certain that students will be seated in a single row, "horseshoe" arrangement so that everyone has an unobstructed view of your chart.
- Use dark color pens
- Use fire colors for highlighting or titles only.

Ensure Excellent Repair, Order, and Cleanliness – "Keep It Shipshape"

It is important that everything is in good working order. Ensure that spaces are neat and clean, and that everything is neatly organized with NO unnecessary clutter, supplies, or other distracters visible to the students.

Protect Your Day
Backup Everything

Batteries

Make sure you have an ample supply of extra batteries, and always put new batteries in your equipment before you start. When our batteries die during instruction, it is always at an inopportune time – don't let this happen to you!

Electrical Equipment

If you will be *dependent* upon computers, overhead projectors, or anything else that could fail, ensure that you will have backup equipment, replacement bulbs, extension cords, and methods of surviving when things go wrong.

Notes, Transparencies, Etceteras

Things do get lost and damaged. Make sure that if your "stuff" disappears or is ruined, you have whatever you will need to teach effectively anyway.

When Providing Instruction Somewhere Else

Take everything you may need that can be carried – don't leave your success in someone else's hands.

Notes

Notes

Even take backups for what you need. In addition, in a workshop setting, ask the people in charge of where you will be teaching to have backup systems, equipment, and supplies available for you. For example we carry everything we might need when we travel except the projectors, screens, tables, and chairs.

Plan for Effective Seating and Tables

Instructional furniture can be arranged in numerous ways to be very effective. However, there are many mistakes that can undermine learning. What follows is a list of principles and tips to facilitate planning an arrangement conducive to learning.

1. Learners should face front. If tables or desks are provided, orient them so that everyone is facing either the front or a direction that is within 45 degrees of the front.

2. Ensure adequate space for learners not to feel cramped.

3. Make sure that whether people are standing or seated, it is easy for them to move around within the room or to either enter or leave the room.

   ■ Round tables tend to be most conducive to group work. Place the seating in a horseshoe arrangement with a limit of five to seven people per table to prevent anyone from not having to turn too much in order to be facing the front. Make certain there is ample space between the tables for easy movement.

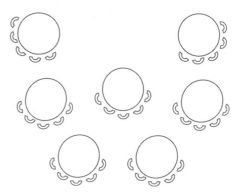

- Rectangular tables should be limited to five to seven people each and set so that no one is facing more than 90 degrees from an "imaginary" line to the front of the room.

- Tables provide effective work space but limit space for movement and mixing.
- Avoid any setting in which tables and chairs are fastened to the floor or each other –Fixed seating prevents adequate movement and flexibility.
- If rectangular tables are used, create chevron patterns or group clusters to facilitate group interaction. This will reduce the problem of people sitting in perfectly straight rows such that

they are looking more at the wall than at the instructional focus point. Ensure ample space between the tables for easy movement.

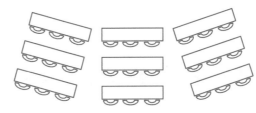

- If the room is set with chairs, often a very appropriate choice because of the flexibility for movement and grouping, start with curved rows open to the front. As with tables, allow plenty of room for movement. The chairs should be at least six inches apart to avoid the "sardine effect." Also, include extra aisles between sets of chairs to allow ease of entry and exit to and from the chairs.

Notes

Page 31

Notes

■ If possible, arrange the room so there is extra room in the front half for tables and/or chairs and open space in the back for activities requiring a lot of movement.

Plan Your Teaching Area

Splurge with Your Space

Give yourself more table space for your instructional materials than you believe you will need. Take the time to spread out your materials in a very neat, organized way for your thinking and working patterns.

Remove Barriers

Place your table for presentation equipment and supplies so that its longest dimension is front-to-back in the room. This allows you to stand in front with your equipment without a barrier between you and your students.

Plan Students' Work Area

Enable students' learning and remove unnecessary barriers by ensuring that your students will have everything they may need while they are working.

Student Supplies

Determine all the possible supplies that your students might need. Then, either arrange them neatly on their work surfaces or develop a plan for their distribution that will provide opportunities for the students to be up and moving. Make sure the supplies are very neatly held in containers within reach of each student. Sample supplies can include:

■ Colored pens – have one of each needed color for each student
■ Post-It notes – multiple sizes, colors, and packages are helpful
■ Index cards – several for each student in multiple colors
■ Scissors
■ Straight edges and rulers
■ Glue
■ Pens and correction fluid or tape
■ Pencils and erasers
■ Tape – masking and/or scotch tape
■ Handouts

Page 32

Trash Buckets

Place containers to serve as trash buckets on each student group's table for scrap paper, wrappers, or any other trash that may be generated. This facilitates keeping the work areas neat at all times. Sandbox pails and cardboard, disposable paint buckets work very well for this purpose.

The trash buckets will need to be emptied regularly, and, periodically, they may require washing or replacement.

Nutrition Stations for Nutritious Snacks

Make certain that there are nutritious snacks (proteins and complex carbohydrates tend to work best) placed on the students' work tables or on a special table designated as the nutrition station.

Helpful Hints

Limit sugars. Provide for diverse needs such as those of diabetics and vegetarians.

Hydration Station for Water

Have drinking water available on the students' work tables or at a special "hydration station."

Room Selection and Preparation

The room should be bright and cheerful. Avoid dark colors. Open the shades (we certainly hope there are ample windows for natural light) and turn up the lights. If the lighting is fluorescent, keep the lights on, but try to balance them with incandescent lamps. When students walk into the room, the immediate feeling should be one of uplifting, energizing excitement – just as one feels when stepping outdoors for a breath of fresh air.

Be careful of walls or curtains that feel dark or heavy – they will act like magnets drawing your students' energy. Do whatever you can to keep students from looking into shadowy, dark areas – try using posters and lamps to lighten up and brighten the room.

Protect yourself also; if you are looking into a dark area while you are teaching, it will drain your energy.

Ample space is important. Though it isn't always possible, we recommend at least 40 square feet per person. This provides enough space for flexible seating, instructional and audiovisual supplies and equipment, and still allows for group activities with movement and standing.

Notes

Page 33

Notes

Wall space is also important but not at the expense of natural light. Walls are critical for displaying posters representing critical concepts and displaying student work. They also are important for processing activities such as gallery walks and carousel graffiti.

Eliminate sound distractions. If noisy equipment is near or in your instructional space, do all that you can to remove it or have it turned off during instruction. Noise pollution is irritating and interferes with students' ability to hear and concentrate.

Remove any "stuff" that is not necessary for instruction from the room or neatly stack and store it out of the way of all activities and out of the line of sight of your learners. If the "stuff" can't disappear from sight, at least get it to the back and stored as neatly as possible.

Use specific areas of the room for specific purposes. There should be areas for AV/instructional supplies and materials, learners' supplies, resource materials, nutritional supplies, and water. It is also important to have specific wall locations for visuals such as announcements, assignments, inspirational posters, and organizational information.

Ensure an adequate flow of fresh air without causing your students to get chilled or too warm. People tend to lose energy when the air starts is too warm or stuffy. But beware. If the air is too chilly, students will shut down just as quickly.

Bottom line, when the learners are in the room, they should be able to describe it as a bright, positive, pleasant, functional, neat, well-organized, comfortable place for learning.

Planning Successful Lessons

Successful approaches to teaching effective lessons are numerous. However, lessons that work exceptionally well are usually designed with the following critical components.

1. Develop a clear understanding of your learners, their needs, perspectives, biases, learning styles, backgrounds, points of pride, and "hot buttons."

2. Determine specifically what the students are to learn. This requires identifying exactly what you need to observe from the learners to be certain they have met your learning expectations. Design an activity that will provide you with this needed evidence of successful learning. Be clear as to whether you need

awareness, understanding, a skill or application of a skill, a change in beliefs, enthusiasm for more, or whatever. Your decision here should drive ALL the rest of your plans and the decisions you will have to make on your feet as you monitor and adjust. Develop a fallback or minimum level of expectations, so that you can adjust mid-lesson if the need arises yet still make a successful forward step during your instruction in case your initial expectations prove to not be attainable.

3. Determine in advance the benefits that the learners will believe they will gain as a result of meeting your expectations. These will help you develop the right "framing" for your lesson.

4. Determine multiple strategies for providing instruction to ensure your expectations are met. Keep in mind these strategies should allow you to successfully and seamlessly drop to your fallback expectations if necessary. Be certain that the strategies will result in observable behaviors by the learners that match the behaviors called for by the verbs in the statements of your learning expectations.

5. Develop "Concepts-on-the-Wall" posters relating the major concepts you will be teaching. These posters need to:

- Be large enough so that they can be easily interpreted from every possible student location in the room.
- Be written with easy-to-read fonts and/or interpreted graphics.
- Use the least number of words possible to represent the main idea.
- Incorporate any icons, graphics, or pictures that will help convey the concept.
- Use effective colors (usually dark) for easy reading and interpretation from distances.
- Use colors consistently. The color used in a poster to represent a concept should match the color used for that concept in any other visuals being used.
- Placed such that the most important concepts are toward the

Notes

Notes

front, and emotional and motivational concepts toward the rear. Wall space should be left at the rear of the room for student-generated work.

6. Plan both the strategies and techniques that will most likely be needed for ensuring an effective physical and emotional context.

7. Plan to teach all procedures (such as for bringing the group back together) before you use them. (Please refer to *Procedures, Procedures, Procedures*, page 47)

8. For any strategies, develop effective plans for teaching and guiding each step.

9. Develop effective emotional, physical, and conceptual transitions to be utilized throughout the execution of the lesson.

10. Develop opening comments and activities that will:

   ■ provide learners with a clear picture of what they are to learn,

   ■ begin developing positive relationships with the learners, and
   ■ result in them believing they will benefit from the learning.

11. Be prepared to drop back and lower resistance before beginning with your planned agenda.

12. Include in your plans, the strategy you will use to cause the learners to debrief or unpack their learning experiences.

13. Practice your comments, strategies, and techniques before you try them with your students. It is best to practice with people who will help by providing reasonable challenges by pretending to struggle with what you are doing.

Part Three

Starting Successful Lessons

Techniques that Smooth the Way Before the Students Arrive

Notes

Dress for Respect and Success

Show respect for your students and earn their respect at the same time by dressing one to two steps above (but no more) your students. Never dress as they do (unless they are dressed in suits), and never appear pretentious by dressing more than two steps above them. Dressing with layers that allow for quickly shifting from professional to smart, professional casual allows for quick, easy shifts as needed.

Arrive Very Early to Ensure Success

It is important to complete all setup before the students arrive. This provides ample time to greet the students as they arrive. We usually arrive for our teaching and training sessions at least one and one half to two hours ahead of time. It takes this much time to plan the room, adjust the tables and chairs, hang posters, appropriately setout all the supplies, adjust the audio-visual equipment, and organize our teaching area. Even if we are able to setup the night before, we still arrive early enough to double check everything.

Orient the Room

Check the room for lighting, lightness of walls, noise and visual pollution, and anything else that could affect your learners. Adjust the room as necessary to ensure the best possible orientation for their learning without distractions or facing dark, energy-drawing areas.

Verify Spacing with a Quick Walk About

Actually test the spacing in the room with all the chairs pulled back from any tables and make any adjustments necessary so that all your students will be able to come and go easily and will be able to get up and move around without any traffic jams.

Display Major Concepts on the Wall

On the walls, place posters (see the criteria for these posters in the section *Planning Successful Lessons*) that convey the major concepts you are there to teach and that will help to build positive relationships with your students. Make sure that the posters are:

- High enough so they can be seen over the heads of other students but not so high as to be out of a natural line of sight.
- Placed in relationship to each other such that they are logically arranged for conceptual interpretation. Consider your wall space to be like pages in a book – make it tell your story.
- Arranged on the walls in the same order (front-to-back, left-to-right) in

Notes

Notes

which they will appear in any other visuals.

- Very neatly and evenly displayed on the walls.

Align Projection Equipment

- Make sure any screens are raised to their highest position so your students can see the images over others' heads.
- Carefully clean the lenses and other surfaces of your projectors.
- Pick up overhead projectors by the base only – never by the arms.
- Adjust any projectors so their images fill the screen and are parallel with the screens edges. The top edges of your images should be in line with the top edge of the screen.
- With overhead projectors, use tape to mark the lowest point on the transparency table below which your transparencies won't be visible over the heads of students.
- Replace any projector bulbs that are burned out or which project a yellowish, not bright white, image. The yellowish color indicates the bulb is near the end of its life. Yellow bulbs are significantly dimmer than new ones.

- Check your projected images from everywhere a student might be. Remember to do this while holding your hand in front of your face to represent the heights of other students' heads.

Note: If an unavoidable visibility problem exists, show you care by apologizing to the students and expressing your appreciation for their understanding.

Adjust the Lighting

Strive for the brightest, natural lighting possible without having direct sunlight in your students' eyes. Open the blinds and shades. Turn on all the lights.

Eliminate Distracting Noises

Find any possible sources of distracting noises from equipment or other sources. Eliminate or reduce these noises – they will distract and annoy your students.

Check Microphones and Other Sound Systems

- Make sure that all sound systems are clear, adjusted to the appropriate volume and tone for your group, and appropriately set to be free from distortion and feedback.

- Check for the volume levels of your voice and music amplification to reduce student discomfort and frustration caused by not being able to hear easily or by having the sound so loud that it hurts their ears. Be prepared to warn some students that they may need to block or cover the ears at certain times – show you understand and that you care.

The Last Minute "Straighten Up"

Walk the entire instructional area. Straighten, organize, and clean anything your most "neat-nik" student might think should be addressed.

As Your Students Arrive

Have Music Playing as Your Students Arrive

Play upbeat music at a comfortable volume for conversation as your students are entering the classroom. This will provide a safety zone for conversations while providing a pleasant atmosphere. Though it's almost impossible to find music everyone likes, try to select something that will have a positive effect on their moods – we find that rock and roll from the late fifties and very early sixties tends to work best with students of just about all ages.

Greet Students as They Arrive

Either greet the students as they enter or make a point of wandering the room welcoming people. Look for students who are potentially resistors and do what you can to make a positive personal connection.

Let Them Be in the Back and with Their Friends – for Now

Wherever your students choose to sit as they initially enter the room, let them. If they're in the back, and you would prefer them closer, don't fight the battle now, you will lose. At this time, focus on positive connections. Then, after you have started, in a light, welcoming, connecting way, appeal to the whole group to move forward on your command (using your direction's *Launch Button, page 50*). This technique of waiting and asking all at once will create a huge wave of willing students moving forward in such a way that they can maintain their relative front-to-back positioning. An added benefit to this technique is that it makes it harder for others to resist.

Notes

Notes

In the Beginning

Visualize Success

Before starting your instruction, pause and visualize yourself and your class. Force yourself to see yourself teaching, but focus most on the learners. See in your mind's eye what you want to be happening. Whatever it is, laughter, excitement, or deep engagement and involvement, see the learners doing it and see what you're doing to cause it. Then, as you are engaged in instruction, remember the vision, compare it to what you're getting, and make whatever adjustments you need.

Connect in 90 Seconds

Make a personal connection within the first 90 seconds. This can be done through a socially appropriate joke, relevant story, or the sharing of your commitment to meet your students' needs. Make a good, positive first impression by either sharing of yourself or your sincere desire to give to them.

Apologize and Express Appreciation Quickly If Anything Isn't Right

Don't let problems fester. Show your concern for your students quickly by acknowledging anything that they might believe is not right. At the same time, let them know that you and the other planners worked hard to do all that you could and will continue to look for ways to solve the problems. Don't forget to also thank your students for their patience and understanding.

Provide Agendas Upfront – Let Students Know Your Agenda Quickly

Use your judgment as to when to get this in, but remember some students need to know the outcomes and/or general agenda very early in the learning process. Be sure to use language the students will understand and state the information in ways the students will immediately see a value in their time being spent with you.

Foster Positive Anticipation

Either with a question or with carefully planned inflections and pauses, have the students generate the potential benefits to them that came from their engagement in your teaching.

Ensure Safety

Because of people's need for safety, quickly prove to your students that they do NOT need to worry about being embarrassed or getting hurt. Telling people they will be safe is not enough. Our actions will speak louder than words.

Notes

Notes

Part Four

Techniques for Giving Directions that Work

Notes

Procedures, Procedures, Procedures

Take time to teach the procedures that you want your students to follow and use for such functions as:

- When and how to start talking or begin acting on a command such as entering into a discussion in a think-pair-share (See *Launch Buttons*.)
- Leaving for breaks or the end of class
- Going to a restroom
- Getting materials
- Drawing discussions to a close in a think-pair-share
- Handing in work or materials
- Distributing materials

To do this, determine specifically, *step-by-step*, how your students are to carry out your procedures, test your plan, and then take time to teach it.

Consistency, Consistency, Consistency

Be certain to follow your procedures exactly and consistently. If we deviate, students can become confused and will modify as they believe they need to in order to be helpful to you or in order to feel successful. Regardless, when our procedures breakdown, students become at risk for "feeling stupid," and the effectiveness and efficiency of our lessons significantly drops off. Bottom line, *be consistent* with your procedures. Of course to be consistent with sophisticated, effective procedures requires practice, practice, and more practice. Without adequate practice, our procedures will breakdown and our instructional effectiveness will diminish.

Practice, Practice, Practice

Consistency with sophisticated procedures requires adequate practice. Imagine that you have taught your students to draw their discussions to a close when they hear the music start, and imagine that the song you're playing during their discussion ends when you still wanted them to be talking. Now what do you do? Your students will start to wind down their conversation, wonder why you are cutting them short without a warning (which you probably said you would do). No matter what you do, the students will already be on the road to ignoring your directions. Don't let this happen – practice, practice, and practice some more until you have down using your procedures without glitches.

Clarify Desired Responses

When we wish to know who in our class has completed a task, we often ask something like, "Who is finished?" Some students will raise their hands, some will look up, some will speak out, and some students will look confused because they don't know how to respond. If we clarify the signals we desire,

Notes

Notes

we will tend to see better results. Next time, while raising *your* hand, say, "Raise your hand if you are finished."

Avoid saying, "How many of us …?" The students won't be sure what response we want and will guess. This slowly turns over management functions to chaos. It can also lead to students doing something that was not intended and feeling stupid.

Signal Response Closures

When students are asked to raise their hands or perform some other behavior as a signal, they are often not told when it is appropriate to lower their hands. Many students will begin lowering their hands as they decide it is appropriate, but others will often dutifully leave their hands in the air until they begin to grow tired or feel stupid. Protect your students while maintaining your position of power by signaling your response closure. For example, after asking students to raise their hands while modeling the same, signal when it is appropriate to lower their hands by saying, "thank you" while lowering your hand.

Just Say It – Keep it Simple and to the Point

Give directions as concisely and precisely as possible. Instead of saying, "What I would like to ask

you to do is open your books to page 23," just say, "Please open your books to page 23." It takes fewer words, less time, and sends a stronger message.

Clear and Specific Directions

Be very clear and leave no room for interpretation. Use nouns even if you think a pronoun will work.

Say	Don't Say
Get the book.	Get it.
Put the book on the top shelf under the window.	Put it over there.

Make sure your verbals and non-verbals are aligned and saying exactly what you mean. For example, rather than saying, "Please go out the door on the right," say, "Please go out that door" (while pointing to the door you wish them to use). Then follow this command with Directionalizing (see below). The problem with right and left for directions, for example, is they require thought to interpret. If we aren't absolutely clear, there is room to question, "Who's right?"

Directionalize

Tell students the specific place or direction to which you want them to go while pointing to it. Follow the request with something like, "When I say go, point to the door you are to go out." Having the students directionalize with you will ensure that everyone knows which door, correct any misperceptions, and put the knowledge in their bodies – muscle memory is a wonderful tool to use.

Command Presence

When working with students, project a *Command Presence.* It is important that your students see you as a confident, strong leader.

Match your tone of voice, gestures, attire, posture, movement, inflection, and choice of words to the message or directions you are trying to convey. Say it like a friendly sergeant, sound and stand like you mean it.

One-Step-at-a-Time Directions

"What are we supposed to do?" is a question that we probably hear more than we wish after we have given a set of directions to our students. Most of us have probably had the situation occur in reverse when we are students or participants in a class or meeting. Author and speaker, Dr. Rich Allen suggests that we can reduce the "speed bumps" in our classrooms by slowing down and giving directions "one-step-at-a-time." For example, a sequence of *One-Step-at-a-Time Directions* might be something like this.

"Put all your books and papers in a neat stack on your desk."
Wait and watch …

"Raise your hand if someone near you is still stacking his or her books. Thank you."
Wait and watch …

"Put your stack of books and papers under your chair"
Wait and watch …

"Thank you."

And the process continues. At first, it will seem like everything is taking forever, but in the long run, everything will go smoother and faster and produce better results. (*Original Concept Shared by Rich Allen, Lake Tahoe, California*)

"Mother, May I" Directions

A common problem with giving directions is students will often "jump the gun." They start acting on what they think the request will be before all students really know or understand all the directions. Take time to teach procedures for acting on directions. The secret to doing this effectively is to use *Launch Buttons,* teach the behavior of waiting for the *Launch Button,*

Notes

Notes

and reteach the *Launch Button* behavior whenever it is needed.

Direction Launch Buttons

Launch buttons do what their name implies – they cause something to start. Include "*launch buttons*" in directions or instructions that you give students.

- "When I say, 'GO' … put your books under your chair. Get ready, set, go."
- "When the 'music starts,' share with your partner the …" Then start the music.
- "When the "music ends," …"
- "When 'I raise my hand,' …"

Launch buttons should be used in a fast, simple, non-contrived way. Their use needs to be taught, practiced, and revisited regularly to ensure that your instructions and activities run efficiently. *Remember: Be sure to state your launch button every time and then don't forget to use it.*

Activity Closers

"When the music stops, please draw your conversations to a close within about seven seconds." Use signals like this one as ways of gently but firmly managing the closure of your activities. Determine *Activity Closers* that will work well for

you and take the time to teach them as part of teaching your procedures, practice them until you are proficient in their use, and be consistent with them. Avoid having to shout over your students or waiting for what seems forever for your students to close their activity – teach, practice, and be consistent with your activity closing procedures. (Please refer to *Procedures, Procedures, Procedures*, page 47)

Time Warnings

Time Warnings help students to anticipate what will be next, complete their tasks in a timely manner, and find comfort in a well-structured situation. When we provide students with *Time Warnings*, we are providing a structure that helps to ensure that our students' Success and Safety Keys are protected.

Two effective ways to use *Time Warnings* include:

1. *Commencement Time Warnings* – Telling students how long until they will actually commence an activity with the use of a *Launch Button*. "In about 5 seconds, when the music starts, form groups of three to five."

2. *Closing Time Warnings* – Advising students as to the approximate amount of time remaining for a given task. " Please take about 30 more seconds to reach a pausing point."

Page 50

Deep Breaths First

Just before giving directions, ask students to take a deep breath and then to let it out. This will gradually become a signal that directions are about to be given. It will also increase the oxygen flowing in your students' blood and potentially lead to increased understanding of the directions and decreased negative responses.

Do-able Directions

Think through your directions before giving them to ensure they are do-able. Be careful to not accidentally give directions that are either impossible to carry out or that will lead to undesirable situations. For example, if we ask students to talk with the person on their right, it won't work – the students will all turn to the right and find themselves looking at their neighbors' backs. If we ask students to form groups of some exact size, there is always a chance it won't be possible at best, or just as bad, it will be difficult for some students to find partners as groups rapidly form around them.

Bottom line, make sure exact directions are easy to follow quickly to avoid embarrassment or feelings of failure, or provide wiggle room to ensure quick success.

An example of a *Do-able Direction* is …

When I say, "Go," please form groups of two or three. Look around and make sure no one gets left out – a group of four would be OK.

Adjustable Group Sizes

When asking students to form groups, give them a range for the size of the group. This helps groups to form quickly, protects students from being excluded, and helps prevent students from getting stuck with others they don't like. For example, "When the music starts, please form groups of two to three, four is OK but will not be the best for the task we will be doing. Don't forget, don't leave anyone out. Ready, set, form groups of two to three." – Start the music.

Inclusion Directions

Often when groups are forming, several students will feel left out, excluded, or embarrassed because they can't get into a group quickly enough or don't feel comfortable joining with others.

Before launching your students into forming groups, advise them to look around as they are forming groups to bring others into their group who may be near by.

Protection Directions

Before giving directions, determine what fears students might have in carrying them out. Then, add steps to your directions to provide the needed safety

Notes

Notes

for the students, their belongings, or the people around them. For example, use *Protection Directions* like…

- Before we do this next activity, make sure your books will be safe by putting them under your chair when I say go … go.
- For what we're about to do, we will need space, so when I say go, please spread yourselves out so everyone is at least an arms' length away from anyone else … go.
- If you would be uncomfortable engaging in the next activity, please choose to be a process observer. In a moment, we will find out who would like to be our process observers and give them their specific and very important tasks.

Multiple Modality Directions

State complex directions one at a time and in multiple ways for multiple modalities.

Example:

- So the directions for our next activity won't be confusing, we will do them one step at a time. In addition, I will give each one in a couple ways to match different learning styles.
- Please find the cartoon in your booklet that you think is most relevant to the issues we are discussing … determine the cartoon in your booklet that seems most related to what we have been discussing.

Direction Checks

When directions are possibly confusing, or you expect that a couple of students are not paying attention during your directions, ask your students to form groups of two or three and then ask the groups to check to see if everyone has the same understanding of the directions. If still in doubt, direct the groups to form larger groups of two or three groups to check for common understandings. Then, for a last safety check, ask the students to raise their hands if someone near them has a different understanding of the directions – if so, clarify the directions.

Command Directions

Just tell students to do what needs doing, one-step-at-a-time, without extra words, *Launch Buttons*, pauses, or countdowns if they will completely understand and respond correctly.

It is common for instructors learning to be more effective with directions to overload their directions with techniques that are most effective with directions that take time to convey. If just a few words can be used to express what needs to be done, then say it as a command – politely of course.

Examples:

- Stand-up (while gesturing appropriately and speaking with a voice in a low, commanding tone)
- Please sit down
- Push your chairs in
- Open your books to page 27
- Take a seat

Clear and Specific Directions – Use Nouns for Clarity and Keep It Simple

In directions, use clear and specific nouns, not pronouns. Instead of using words like it, there, he, she, them, that, and other vague words, use the exact noun or proper noun – the book, the bookcase, Jim, Becky, or the debate team.

Vague Directions	Clear and Specific Directions
Put the book over there.	Put your book on the top shelf of the bookcase.
When we leave, we will be going out that door.	When we leave, we will be going out the north door. Please point with me to the north door.
Develop a concept map showing what we have been discussing.	Develop a multi-level concept map showing at least four major points from our discussion and the interconnections between them.
Discuss with your group.	With your group, develop a list of possible causes for the ___ from our reading assignment for last night.

Pick Your Battles

When giving directions or commands in a teaching situation, make certain of your timing, audience, and self. It is important to succeed when asking students to do something without them feeling as though they have lost "a battle." Make sure that what you are asking for is something that will be understood and completed without causing anyone to feel stupid, incompetent, or silly.

Notes

Notes

Part Five

Techniques for
Building Positive Attitudes

Notes

Lower Resistance Before Raising Acceptance

If our students are resistant at the beginning, we can't get anywhere until their resistance is lowered. Before trying to teach or convince anyone of anything, we must take whatever steps are necessary to lower any existing resistance. Start by using relationship builders, and avoid issuing rules or creating perceptions of threats. Don't launch into teaching content until your students are open to you and trust you and your intentions. As soon as you see your path clear of resistance, let the teaching begin.

Respect as the Foundation

Immediately start showing sincere respect for each person and group in the classroom. People will not always return respect, but they will almost always return what they believe is a lack of respect.

Relationships are at the Heart

Positive, healthy relationships with our students are not negotiable if we want high performance. People will do almost anything for others who they value enough. Starting with students' first experience, build and maintain strong, positive relationships. It is important to note, however, that in healthy relationships, people are expected to meet standards and they are supported in their progress until the standards are met.

Novelty Balances Structure

Routine and structure are essential for feelings of safety. Without them, learners are likely to become distracted, uneasy, and ineffective students. However, too much routine and structure becomes boring and students have a hard time maintaining engagement. Provide enough structure for students to feel safe and comfortable, but mix it up enough to maintain interest.

Humans are programmed to pay attention to anything different, be it sound, movement, taste, or smell. We are also programmed to begin to drop into a rest state if there is no change occurring. Create changes by varying things just enough to manage student engagement. If we use too much novelty, students do become exhausted and begin to shut down. Manage their engagement through novelty and rest so our learners' energy, attention, and engagement is flowing in well-managed waves.

Recognition

Recognition is highly valued by virtually all people. Call students by name as often as possible. When talking with them, use their names often.

People enjoy being recognized for who they are – show recognition for what each student brings to the class. While providing recognition, remember to say something appropriate and nice to each student every day, but try to make it specific and nonjudgmental.

Notes

Notes

"Jim, your homework is out and ready right on time. Thank you."

The Color of Their Socks

Oftentimes we as teachers have students who are difficult for us to like. Though it is quite normal to not like everyone, we can't let this show with our students or we will lose them. People can usually sense what others are feeling about them – it is hard to cover up negative feelings. A trick to solve this problem is to find *something* about a troubling student that we do like and focus on it, even if it's the color of their socks.

Frames to Make the Picture

A rainy day is neither good nor bad. What is important is our attitude. "Today our flowers are getting water to make them beautiful next week." With whatever is to happen in the classroom, start by creating a positive way to frame it. "Doing well at anything comes with practice. In this course, we will practice, just like in sports, piano lessons, or video gaming, until we all are excelling."

When learners are worried about what is about to happen or whether or not their time is going to be wasted, they begin to shut down, become frustrated or angry. Overcoming negative emotions is difficult at best, and impossible at worst. Why take a chance?

Take the time to create a positive frame by:

1. Making sure you have determined how what happens will be beneficial to your students, and share these benefits with them.

2. Using language and examples that match your students' needs, interests, and preferred ways of being and learning. For example, if you are working with shy introverted people, don't tell them you will be having a lot of fun, playing games, or interacting with groups. Instead let them know that they will be getting something they can use in a way that will be safe and enjoyable for everyone.

Celebrations

Look for, create, and take advantage of opportunities to celebrate what students are doing in your classroom. Keep your celebrations equal for your students. Be certain that you use the same celebration to the same level of intensity with each student or group of students. Pick one celebration method for everything or a separate one for each type of celebration.. Use your celebration rituals every chance that you can.

Inclusive Language

Whenever appropriate, find ways to use words like "us" and "we."

For example, ask:

- "How many of us …?" rather than, "How many of you …?"

- Or, rather than saying, "You are to …", say, "We are going to …"

The use of the word "you" in situations like these just creates an unnecessary barrier in our relationships. After all, aren't great, inspirational leaders always willing to work along side?

Avoid Conversation Blockers

Words like "yes" tend to keep conversations going, and words like "no" tend to block or end conversations.

Answering with words and phrases that promote ongoing conversation is easy when our response is positive, but a challenge otherwise. Avoid saying or implying "no," "you're wrong," or anything else that may be taken as criticism, correction, judgment, manipulation, or control.

Potential *Conversation Blockers* include word and phrases such as:

- No
- Wrong
- You must …
- You should …
- You need to …
- Negative
- No, thank you
- But
- Bless your heart
- Why?
- You (when its use might imply to the listener feelings or experiences actually held by the speaker. For example, someone who is describing skiing to someone else may say something like, "When you are skiing on really steep slope, it scares you." The listener in this case is not and probably has not skied on a steep slope, and in addition, may wonder why the speaker is suggesting that he gets scared.)

Rather than telling students what they *must* do, try telling them what "we are to do." As for "but," rumor has it that it's an acronym for "**b**ehold, the **u**nderlying **t**ruth." When the word "but" is heard in someone's

Notes

Notes

sentence, it usually means that what was just said is not true, the truth is about to follow.

Safety and Success Keys – The Easiest and Fastest to Break

While teaching, constantly ask yourself, "In what is happening, are all of my students feeling safe and successful enough for them not to shut down?" If the answer is not a strong YES, quickly look for adjustments to save the situation before students are lost in the potholes that disrupt the journey to greater knowledge.

Love and Belonging Filters – the Key to Inclusion

People's need for inclusion is strong. Constantly monitor your students for feelings of exclusion. At the first hint that any student does not feel accepted, respected, cared about, included, liked, or like they belong, take action. Avoid any sense of in and out groups on the part of your students. Be careful to use examples and activities that engender feelings of equal respect. For example, teachers who are pereceived as athletic should use non-athletic examples. When asking students to form groups, use adjustable group sizes and remind students to welcome in any students near them looking for a group. Bottom line, build feelings of inclusion.

Control and Manipulation Filters

While teaching, constantly ask yourself, "Are any of my students feeling overly controlled or manipulated?" If the answer to this question is even a maybe, quickly make adjustments to provide meaningful choices and freedom from overly persuasive tactics to keep from losing your students' engagement. Using the control and manipulation filters provides us with the insights we need during the instructional process to protect and use the Freedom and Independence Key.

Fun and Enjoyment Key, the Bottom Line Decision Screen

Monitor your students' enjoyment levels. Do what needs to be done for them to believe that what they are doing is enjoyable enough to be a viable use of their valuable personal resources.

Valued Purpose Key – A Filter for Instructional Decisions

Continuously monitor your students to be certain that the content you are teaching is valuable to your students or that your instruction has created a situation in which your students wish to be engaged. If one of these is not happening, quickly find a way to reframe what you are teaching or how you are doing it. As soon as your students make the decision that there are more worthwhile things for them to be doing with their time and energy, they will be lost until you can gain them back.

Distribution Movement

When students need materials of any kind, you have a great opportunity to get them moving. It may be faster to just distribute whatever is needed, but the benefits of the physical movement on the students' moods, attitudes and engagement is well worth the extra time it takes to have them get up and get their own materials.

Potholes along the Road to Greater Knowledge

Potholes tend to cause aggravation for drivers at best, and at worst, bring an unfortunate end to a drive. When students encounter unnecessary cognitive and emotional dissidence in learning situations, it creates a "jarring" for them that temporarily, and sometimes permanently, blocks learning. Watch out for everything in your teaching that creates a jolt in your learners. These jolts often lead to spontaneous, temporary shutdowns in learning. Eventually if there are too many of them or if they are too significant for the students, they can lead to significant breakdowns in the relationships and the learning.

One way potholes in classrooms differ from those in a road is that the size and impact of the pothole is determined by the students. In other words, what might be a huge pothole to some students may not even be noticeable to others.

Some potential potholes that can shut down learning include:

- If the teacher doesn't tell the students to lower their hands, a student might be embarrassed by discovering her hand is still in the air after others have lowered theirs.
- Students who move the wrong direction when asked to do something.
- Words or stories that create unintentional emotional shocks.
- Directions that are not understood, resulting in students needing to ask, "What are we supposed to do?"
- Students being asked to do something that they can't figure out how to get done.
- Students not being able to form a group quickly because there aren't others immediately near them with whom to group.

Notes

Notes

- Students being given a handout and then not given time to skim it because the teacher just keeps talking.
- Students being caught not having heard a question or direction because they took time to look through a handout that was just distributed.
- Students being asked to stand up and move somewhere else without knowing why or if it will be safe.
- Students finding themselves in activities in which they are being touched or having to touch someone else.
- Students being told to move somewhere without being given a chance to protect their belongings.

Enthusiasm is Contagious

Exude enthusiasm for what you are teaching, the fact that you are fortunate enough to be a teacher, and for the fact you are lucky enough to be your students' teacher. Enthusiasm is contagious. In addition, there is research suggesting it can lead to increased student motivation and learning. So, no matter what is happening, refuse to have a bad day. After all, it is just a day. It's our choice whether or not we choose to journey through it with enthusiasm.

Oxygenization

People become sleepy and disengaged when they are not getting enough oxygen. Use frequent requests for deep breaths and/or frequent opportunities for physical movement to keep the students' circulation active.

Movement

It is uncomfortable to remain seated or standing for too long. Have students move regularly, to keep the blood flowing and to prevent soreness and discomfort.

Congruent Responses

When asked a short, direct question, give a short, direct response. If more explanation is needed, follow your quick answer with something like, "However, there are numerous factors that could impact the situation. Let me explain some other possibilities."

Avoid Asking, Why?

Often times, when people hear the question, "Why?", they experience a slight jolt of cognitive and emotional dissidence – a teaching and learning "pothole." Typically when people are asked a question starting with "why," it is because they did something wrong.

Avoid creating the possible stress which will block or delay learning and engagement and find other ways of phrasing questions, such as:

- What might be the reasons…?
- How come…?
- What could have been possible…?

Timing is Everything

Keep things at a fast and do-able pace to avoid your students feeling bored and frustrated. Downtime is deadly – don't let it happen. Another problem with timing is that students work at different rates. This can lead to students feeling bored if they finish early or incompetent if they are slower than the others – both of which will undermine your teaching efforts.

If an activity requires that everyone finish completely, provide a second phase to the activity that need not be completed. This second phase must be such that when students shift into it, other students will not know the shift is occurring. For example, if the students are to read a paragraph, ask them to read the paragraph and then to continue reading if they finish before time is called – then don't call time until you are certain everyone has finished reading the desired paragraph. Some other possible fillers of time include:

- Ask students to silently record notes, reflections, questions, or insights.
- Fill empty time between the statement of the *Launch Button* and the *Launch Button* with something like, "Ready, get set, 'go'".
- Ask students to create icons, maps, or pictures conveying important thoughts.
- Use *meaningful fillers* and *bridges* – see the following section.

Value Added Bridges – Meaningful Fillers and Transitions

Meaningful fillers and transitions are quick statements and activities that keep things going while providing an effective bridge into what's next without nagging or waiting (while some are getting bored waiting with you) for a group to come back together.

For example, after you have used your cue to end a group activity and there is a significant group of students who are not yet paying attention, direct your students to "Thank your partners." This can then be followed with more bridges such as, "Give your partners a high five." or "Say 'Goodbye' to your partners."

Notes

Notes

Value Added Bridges will gently get the attention of the whole class and provide for a meaningful and polite act, which becomes the smooth bridge to your next statement, activity, or direction.

Music for Transitions

Play upbeat, conversational tone music during transitions unless the students are "on the wild side" and need calming.

Whenever the students are coming or going, entering or exiting, or whenever they are shifting from one activity to another, play music to boost their spirits and energy to keep them awake and happy about being "at school." If they are too much "on the wild side," use baroque music to create the desired calming effect.

Musical Pads – Safety Zones

When students have been asked to engage in conversations, play music in the background at comfortable conversational levels. This provides a "sound" safety zone or "pad" in which their conversations are more private. (Please refer to *Launch Buttons*, page 50, for starting *Musical Pads - Safety Zones*.)

Musical Humor

Use popular music that can add fun and spontaneity. Include music from movies, musicals, game shows, and other television shows to add fun and enjoyment into your teaching. Examples of fun music include:

- The *Jeopardy* Theme
- *Mission Impossible* Theme
- The theme from *Superman*
- *Celebration* by Kool and the Gang
- *William Tell Overture*
- Many songs from Disney movies
- Cartoon themes

Another fun way to use music is to look for word connections between the first lines of the music to the activities or questions you are doing with your students. For example, you could use "North to Alaska" by Johnny Horton when teaching about Alaska, or you could use "Raindrops keep falling on my head…" for a science lesson on weather or for a meeting regarding problems that need solving.

Juke Box Break

Set aside a time in every class, week, or day for the students to take turns selecting the music. Require the music to be pre-approved based on community values and expectations which need to be clarified before students begin making selections.

Dignity Protection for Awkward Situations – We're Not Alone

Standing out in a crowd is desirable for many people, but when it's for reasons they consider to be negative or potentially embarrassing, it will almost always lead to trouble. Take precautions to protect students from feeling alone in their perspectives or fears.

Here are some tips for solving the problem.

- "Raise your hand if you know others who feel the same way."
- "Say, 'Yes!' if you are like me and are uncomfortable in cooperative learning structures or activities."
- "Tell others in your group why some people might be uncomfortable doing …"
- "Hold your pencil in the air if you are like me and find it uncomfortable when you are expected to sing, dance, or engage in any outgoing behaviors in classes."

After providing this evidence that "we are not alone" with our fears, discomforts, or attitudes, then one additional step can help significantly. Add, "Well, in this class, no one will be forced or manipulated into doing something they are uncomfortable doing. I will do my best to make sure we are all safe, but if at anytime I ask you to do something that is uncomfortable, just use our *Opting Out Signal* (see below) and engage in some other productive use of your time. Please make sure others around you know how and why we will keep each other safe in this class."

Opting Out – the Learners' Protection to Ensure Safety, Autonomy, and Success

Not every activity or situation is appropriate for every learner. Forcing or manipulating students into engaging in activities that they consider unsafe, manipulative or a waste of their time will usually not solve any problems. It will often lead to anger and increased motivation for withdrawal or retaliation.

Provide a safe procedure for students to opt out of activities if they are not feeling safe. We have students put their hand up like they are taking an oath to indicate that they will be sitting out of an activity. When students give the opting out signal, make eye contact and let them know privately through nonverbals that it is OK. When you can find the time, connect with the students, reassure them, help them to engage in another positive activity, and determine what the issue is so that you can work toward them engaging in future activities.

Notes

Notes

Defend My Position

When presenting positions that your students may disagree with, ask them to determine reasons why others might support the position. Let your students know you are *not* expecting them to agree with the position, you are only asking them to develop possible arguments that could be made for the position. In a non-confrontational way, this technique will often result in the students agreeing with the position that they initially opposed.

Ask, Don't Tell

People are more likely to believe and support that which they generate themselves than what they are told by others. Avoid presenting positions that are contrary to your students' beliefs.

When it is desired for students to develop or change a belief, use questions and activities that will result in the students generating the position for themselves. For example, many classroom teachers would take a negative stance if we were to state, "When standards are really important, students should be held accountable for meeting them through multiple parallel assessments with supportive coaching strategies until the standards are met." However, if we were to put them into various groups representing athletic and drama coaches, business and military trainers, and parents teaching their children to drive and use the "Ask, Don't Tell" technique, we would meet with little opposition. All we would have to do is first ask them to identify some important objectives that might need to be taught in each situation represented, and then ask them to determine likely approaches that would be used to teach them. The problem now will not be one of acceptance for the position statement, the problem will be addressing all the management and other "reality" questions.

Sanctity Protection

For each learner, there are things that are of major importance. Whatever these are, they must be valued and protected by the teacher or the student will begin to shut down.

1. Personal belongings: Always provide ways and means for students to make sure their personal belongings, work, or projects will be safe before engaging the students in any activity. Make certain that students have space for their belongings to be safe.

2. Work and projects: If students are going to be doing anything to one another's work or projects as part of an activity, make certain this is known up front to avoid unnecessary

and very jolting "potholes" in the learning journey for many students.

3. Space: Provide for sufficient space around each student so that the instructional activities will not result in students intruding into each others' space.

4. Self: Students need to believe that they, their space, beliefs, and valued relationships will not be in any way endangered or violated.

Notes

Notes

Part Six

Questioning Techniques that Work

Notes

_____

About Questioning Techniques

Well-developed questions can lead to powerful learning experiences. Good questions promote meaningful and extended probing of our students' minds. Unfortunately, too many questions asked in teaching situations unintentionally accomplish very little. At worst, poorly developed or timed questions can actually shut down learning for students.

Questioning should be used extensively to cause learning, not to catch the students with right and wrong answers. Effective questions result in the students either individually or collaboratively probing their existing knowledge while building new insights or deepening and extending understanding.

Questions that result in students giving incorrect answers can actually result in other students learning wrong information. At the same time, the incorrect student will often feel stupid or embarrassed or both, and the result can be a very negative, counterproductive time in the classroom.

When using questioning as an instructional tool, constantly screen the questions and responses with the Safety and Success Keys' filters to make sure students stay engaged and learning.

Questions to Promote Thinking

Design questions so they show the thinking processes and/or the extent of the students' knowledge or understanding. This allows us to assess the effectiveness of our instruction while generating deeper knowledge or building greater retention. Questions that do this tend to be open-ended. In addition, the questions that have the most positive effect on learning are worded such that they can create the desired growth in knowledge while not generating or exposing poor thinking.

Example stems include:

- What might be the benefits of…?
- How could someone possibly approach this problem?
- What are important similarities and differences that could have…?
- What might be the consequences of…?
- How might others argue on behalf of…?
- What could be three to five defendable reasons to support _____ as _____?

Notes

Notes

Just in Time Questions for Correct Reasoning and Responses – Ask No Question before It's Time

If the purpose of questions is to generate thinking and learning, then the real issue is the quality and the timing of the question. If questions are generating poor responses, then they are either worded poorly or being asked before the students are ready to engage in them.

Use Teaching Questions – Avoid Questions with Strictly Right and Wrong Answers

Questions that result in strictly right and wrong answers, questions probing for recall or correct application of an algorithm, are questions that can catch students being wrong. Though this certainly adds a level of public accountability, the downside of what happens is probably not worth it. When a student is publicly wrong, there will be an emotional response – a "pothole" along the road to greater knowledge. Let this happen too much or at the wrong time for any student, and it's just a matter of time until she will either disengage, misbehave, or take action against us.

Processing Questions

At the end of each point, discovery, process, procedure, event, or project – or at least every ten to fifteen minutes, engage students in questions that will build, extend, or reinforce learning.

- What points were made?
- What steps did we follow?
- How was _____ done?
- How might _____ be important?
- How might someone use _____?
- When could someone use _____?
- What are items that can be listed about _____?
- How might someone describe _____?
- How might people feel about _____?
- What might be the benefits of _____?
- How could _____ be improved?
- What might be cautions with ___?
- How might you do _____ even better?
- What might be good reasons for doing what we did?

Answer Pass-Off

There is a way to protect the students' Safety and Success Keys while asking questions that may result in public exposure of an incorrect response. *Answer*

Pass-Off is the technique through which we have students "pass-off" their answers or give the answers of others.

- How might someone *else* do this problem?
- What approaches might *others* use?
- What are some understandings of _____ that may exist in this class?
- If I were to ask *others*, what would *they* probably say?

Borrowed Answers

Put students into groups to generate possible responses to a question requiring meaningful engagement or exploration. Then have them share in new groups or in front of the whole class what they heard said in response to the question. Ask the students not to identify who said what they are reporting out, just share the response they heard. This will allow students to share their answers if they wish, but they may also share others' answers. In any case, there is no public exposure of a student being wrong, students are simply sharing what they heard.

Notes

Notes

Part Seven

Techniques for Improving the Effectiveness of Teaching Strategies

Notes

Audiences

With all things students are asked to do, no matter how big or small, find ways to provide an audience for their efforts. The more authentic and/or important the audience is for the students, the greater the positive effect will be. This can range from "share what you think with a neighbor" to "present your findings and recommendations" to an exploratory meeting of the state senate.

Mental Gyrations

As often as feasible, stop sequential learning activities and insert *Mental Gyrations* with the content the students are receiving, discovering, or developing. In these *Mental Gyration* breaks, have the students do any of the following with what they are learning or with the new learning mixed with other knowledge they already have.

- Compare _____ with _____ .
- Contrast _____ with _____ .
- Prioritize _____ .
- Put all that we have _____
  into _____ categories.
- Develop a classification system for
  _____ .
- Determine which of _____
  is/are the easiest, best, most
  valuable, or whatever.
- Summarize _____ .

- Determine the most important three to five points out of the
  _____ we developed.
- Develop a defense for the claim that
  _____ is better, worse, more important, useful, a waste of time, relevant, or whatever.
- Determine what other processes you know are similar to this new one.
- Develop a concept map showing how all we've learned is interrelated.

Metaphors and Similes

Metaphors and similes help to create lasting mental images and emotional connections that accelerate learning and increase retention. They are effective for improving learning whether we use them or ask the students to develop them – though clearly having students generate them will have a very large impact because of who is doing the processing. One of the reasons they are so essential as a technique in teaching is that they correspond to the way humans think and remember – forming connections to what we already know, can do, and understand.

Metaphors are figures of speech in which a trait, quality, or name is attributed to something to which it is not truly applicable. For example, "what we are about to go through will prove to be a very (thorny/sticky/slippery/chilling/branching – pick the metaphor that will create the best picture for clarifying what is

Notes

_____

_____

_____

_____

_____

_____

_____

_____

_____

_____

_____

_____

_____

_____

_____

_____

_____

_____

_____

_____

_____

_____

Page 77

Notes

to happen) process."

Similes are also figures of speech that add mental clarity through connections to dissimilar pre-existing knowledge. For example,

- "The functions with this software are as slick as ice."
- "This presentation style is as cold as ice."
- "A good presentation is built like a tower of wooden blocks."
- "The organization of an essay is like that of a cheeseburger."

When we are able to naturally fill our instruction with metaphors and similes, presenting sticky topics becomes a piece of cake and the students find what we have taught to be crystal clear! (We apologize for any discomfort caused by the use of clichés to make our point.)

Analogies

Interjecting plenty of opportunities for students to explore or develop analogies is a powerful technique for accelerating and deepening learning. Analogies build on the power of metaphors and similes, but can go much further through the complex *Mental Gyrations* that can be required of our students. Asking students to develop analogies requires that

they identify the similarities that exist between two (or perhaps more) "things" that are similar in numerous ways but not all – and of course, the technique becomes even more powerful if we ask the students to defend their findings. For example, we could ask students to develop an analogy relating the teaching and assessment practices used by a police academy in teaching how to direct traffic with those used by what might be perceived as a typical algebra teacher. Another analogy that we could use would be the similarities that could be found between solar systems, hurricanes, and atoms.

Brain Writing or Think Time

Before having students share openly or in groups, whether for brainstorming or a processing question, always provide at least seven to ten seconds of time for students to generate and record a response in their mind or notes. This greatly enhances both the quality and quantity of the responses provided by the students, while at the same time, significantly increases the percentage of students who actually engage.

Beneficial Blurting

We know that when students blurt responses to questions, it can stifle the learning of others. Turn blurting into a fun game in the classroom. Tell the students to prepare during *Brain Writing* time to prepare to shout their response – when you push your launch button. Then say, "When I say go, shout your answers to your partners … go!"

Borrowed Questions

Asking students if there are questions tends to be disappointing at best and a boring disaster at worst. Many students do not want to ask questions and appear stupid in front of the group. Others become bored as they listen to questions and answers they don't care about.

Solve the problem by asking students to generate one or two questions that others in the classroom might need answering. Bottom line: Avoid the common trap that many instructors fall into. Don't ask if there are any questions. Ask what questions people might need answering.

Question Cards

Ask your students to list one to three questions on index cards that they believe may need to be answered for the class. Ask students in groups of two or three to share the questions, eliminate any duplicates and questions for which the group quickly decides on an answer. Collect the remaining questions and study them between classes or during a break. When class resumes, thank the students for their questions and share with the class that you are using them to guide the class. As appropriate, read a

question and either answer it or ask the students to answer based on what has just recently happened in class that should provide some important insights. This is also a useful technique for planting questions yourself that you wish to interject into your lessons.

Question Collections

Rather than answering one question at a time, maintain a more effective flow and order by collecting all the questions at once, then determining the best way to approach them. This saves a lot of time while providing more effective instruction. It also helps to reduce student frustration because everyone sees all the questions will be addressed eventually.

Question Reductions

When having students generate questions, have them share their questions in groups. Have the groups develop one or two questions from their set that are most important. This will reduce and refine the questions while actually increasing learning through the process. Also, students will automatically reduce the number of questions in their groups by answering some of them.

Cartoon Connections

Locate cartoons that can in any way be connected to the content you are teaching. Periodically, put up a cartoon and ask the students to collaboratively

Notes

_____
_____
_____
_____
_____
_____
_____
_____
_____
_____
_____
_____
_____
_____
_____
_____
_____
_____
_____
_____
_____
_____
_____
_____
_____
_____
_____
_____
_____
_____
_____
_____
_____

identify all the ways the cartoon connects a concept or skill you are teaching or all the ways it represents an opposite concept, skill, or perspective.

Engagement Opportunities

The more that students are engaged in the learning, the better they will learn. Engage your students through questions, processing, or activities at least every couple minutes. Even rhetorical questions thrown out to the students are better than having the students just watch, listen, or copy.

Follow Through with Closure

A common mistake is to think that when students have heard, done, seen, or experienced something, that they have learned it. Until they can put "it" into their own words and identify benefits or applications, they haven't learned it and it will be quickly forgotten. Before beginning your instruction, identify exactly what you want your students to know, do, and understand. Develop a question or activity that will articulate this predetermined learning in some form, and then, before the students leave after instruction, make certain they articulate what they've done and applications or benefits of it. Just because students experience, do, listen to, or engage in something, doesn't mean they've learned it.

Instant Starts

Down time for students is deadly – it potentially leads to boredom, anger, frustration, and loss of control. Use *Instant Starts* to ensure that as soon as class begins or you've given a signal, you will start **immediately.** During the time that students are engaged with tasks or questions, prepare for an *Instant Start* when you bring the students back together. Before using any signal to begin, make absolutely certain you have all your materials, music, words, or whatever ready to go.

Bottom line, don't bring the students back to attention until you are ready to fly into your next phase, question, or activity. When we don't begin immediately after bringing students back together, we undermine our own classroom management. After all, why should students give us their attention when we signal it if we aren't going to start right away. Who wants to hurry to wait?

Wave Management

While students are learning, monitor their attention and energy levels and use *re-energizers* as needed to manage the wave within the classroom.

Deliberately introduce novelty, use *Squeeze and Release*, employ movement and energizers, and incorporate *Feedback Opportunities* to manage the waves of energy, engagement, and student attention. If invisible outsiders could monitor the students' involvement with the learning in our classrooms, they should see a well-managed "wave pattern" in our students' behaviors, energy use, and engagement. Our observers would see our students hit peaks of energy and mental engagement followed by a deliberate dropping of intensity before we would then begin bringing them back up.

When teachers overuse novelty, voice changes, movement, and activities to keep learners totally and constantly engaged, the students become exhausted and lose interest. If *everything* is important enough for all this then nothing is really important. If teachers don't create pulsing waves of engagement, the classroom becomes boring and the students will become sleepy, bored, disinterested, or exhausted and disengaged.

Re-energizers

Re-energizers are what we use to manage the energy level and mood within our classrooms for wave management.

Re-energizers are typically quick activities that involve movement and a significant change from what has been happening. Monitor the students and use a re-energizer whenever it is apparent that they appear to need a change to maintain their engagement.

Examples:

- If the students have been standing long enough to start to look uncomfortable, have them sit or walk and do something.
- If the students have been sitting, have them move.
- If the students have been listening, have them converse.
- If the students have been working very hard, engage them in a game or other activity they will consider fun.

Squeeze and Release

When students are intently listening or mentally engaging with the content, use pressure releasing process questions and activities to enhance learning. Plan on a release after every point is covered or every ten to fifteen minutes – whichever occurs first. Without it, much of what you are trying to teach will be forgotten long before your students leave the room. Often times the concept of *Squeeze and Release* is referred to as the *Ten-Two Rule*, when in actuality, it is a more sophisticated, student-centered approach to the need of learners to process more regularly.

Notes

Notes

Ten – Two Rule

Since most people can only retain up to about ten minutes worth of new knowledge, they need processing breaks about every ten minutes. The rule suggests providing about two minutes for the students' mental engagement with the content about once every ten minutes.

Seed and Tease

Before your students leave for a break or at the end of a class or day, tell them what they can expect when you reconvene. Do it as enticingly as you can. Also, throughout your teaching, wherever possible, throw out as many enticers, hints, and important tidbits as you can. Make sure that before you ever get to teaching something, it has been referenced in numerous ways several times.

All at Once

Within your first lesson in a course, day of professional development, or segment of a presentation, make sure your learners are exposed to the one or two really big ideas that are crucial to all that they are to learn. In a writing class, the big idea might be the effect with an audience. In an algebra class, it might be about balance and relationships. By gaining the *big idea* early, students have a place to "hang" information as they acquire it.

Frequent Feedback

Feedback is often confused with criticism or a critique. Criticism is what is provided to a learner by someone else. Feedback is internal and provided by the individual. It is what we receive when we are parallel parking a car and either feel the car gliding in just right, notice we are out too far from the curb, or hear the tires screeching on the curb. Feedback is also what we experience as we taste test the food we are cooking. Feedback is the safe and effective way that we determine the correctness of what we are thinking or doing.

Regular feedback is critical to learning!

Opportunities for feedback need to be provided at least once every ten to twelve minutes or after every new point or discovery. It is provided by ensuring the students can check the correctness of what they are thinking through engagement in group conversation, sharing, or individual or group engagement in a task or activity. Feedback can also occur as students self-assesses their work against criteria.

Examples:

1. After the teacher explains something, she can ask pairs of students to share what they think was said in their own words. Each student can then check

his or her understanding by comparing with what the other person has said.

2. After a teacher models a step in a procedure, he can ask the students to replicate what he did and then compare it to what is on the board.

3. After a student demonstrates a skill, she watches a video of the demonstration and compares her performance to the criteria (rubric) and other demonstrations she has seen.

4. After an instructor presents something, the students are asked in groups to share possible interpretations, benefits, applications, examples, or counter examples.

5. Students can read several examples of outstanding opening paragraphs and compare them to their own.

6. Athletes can compare their "moves" on video with videos of other outstanding athletes.

7. Anglers receive feedback regarding their accuracy every time they cast.

Pause for Visual Distractions

Whenever students are given a handout, asked to look at something, or presented with a new chart, overhead transparency, slide, or map, give them time to scan it. Many students will do it anyway and ignore any teacher who is marching on. The students who don't care about what is being taught will want to ignore the visual. Don't give them the opportunity. Provide the pause by saying something like, "Let's take about twenty seconds to look over this chart to see what it might be saying."

Tactile Pacifiers

Many learners struggle if they don't have something they can do with their hands. There are numerous options to help, some of which include:

- Meaningless, repetitive, doodling
- Fuzzy balls
- Pens and pencils

Be careful of toys and crafts that require or promote concentration on them rather than just providing for movement with the hands.

Notes

_____

Page 83

Notes

Stories as Connectors and Enhancers

Use very short stories and parables to make lasting points and connections. After each block of instruction, lesson, or major point, a story can provide a memory hook to boost retention and add value.

Evaluations and other Administrative Functions

Don't let evaluations and other management paperwork and issues take away from important instruction and important times for emotional experiences. Distribute evaluation forms before the last break so that they can be completed before the end of your session. Let your students know they will be there to be completed before the break is over. If evaluations must be done at the end, conduct a powerful ending and then turn your session or lesson over to time for administrative functions.

End with Power

End on an emotional high to add lasting power to your teachings. Use stories, metaphors, song, or any means of drawing closure to your message in a deeply positive and emotional way.

Part Eight

General Techniques for Improving Teaching Effectiveness

Notes

Podiums – NOT Lecterns

Podiums are raised platforms on which a presenter or teacher can stand. Lecterns are furniture stands for speakers' notes. Do not stand behind lecterns; they create unnecessary barriers between the instructor and the students.

Stand on a podium whenever it is necessary to maintain eye contact with every student. It is important to be able to make eye contact at all times. If the students are taller than you are when they are up and moving, stand on something – any box, table, or band directors' platform will do.

Deep Voices

Many people will unintentionally raise the pitch of their voices when teaching a group. Don't. It can sound condescending, it's harder to understand, and it can lead to decreased credibility.

Positive Statements

Tell your students what you want them to do, NOT what you don't want. It's hard for people to respond directly to a negative direction. When we give negative commands, students will very often do just what we don't want.

Positive Statement	Negative Statement to Avoid
Go out the door in the back.	Don't go out the front door.
Look up.	Don't look down.
Be on time.	Don't be late. Or, Try not to be late.
Look at your own work.	Don't look around. Or, don't look at anyone else's work.
Control your emotions.	Don't lose control of your emotions.
Wait until the bell rings.	Don't waste time and get up to leave early.
Run toward the goal.	Do NOT run the wrong direction.

Notes

_____
_____
_____
_____
_____
_____
_____
_____
_____
_____
_____
_____
_____
_____
_____
_____
_____
_____
_____
_____
_____
_____
_____
_____
_____
_____

Notes

Dedicated Instructional Regions

Select specific regions of your classroom to use for each specific function you will perform during instruction. The region in the front of the room is good for presenting information or providing direct instruction. To increase awareness and attention, step into your students. Set aside a spot to the side of your classroom for stories and another spot for general correction or criticism.

Emphasis Movements

Shift your position and stance to physically note a switch in topic or point.

Open and Straight Stance

Face your students straight on. Many people will subconsciously negatively interpret any stance or sitting position that is not straight on. Also, open your stance by keeping your hands and arms outward, not closed in front. Try to keep your hands open, and when your hands are up, a palms up position tends to be interpreted better than when the palms are down.

Auditory Bold – Pauses and Volume Shifts for Emphasis

Whenever shifting to a new point or introducing a word with which your students are not familiar, pause slightly to catch your students' attention and alert them that something is coming that may require

attention. Then say the word of phrase with slightly raised volume and sharpened enunciation to ensure the students are with you.

Value-Added Activities

Collect a set of stories, activities, and process questions that can be used whenever your students are not back and ready to begin learning when you expected them to be. These will allow you to start on time and honor those that are with you and ready to begin while adding value to what is being learned. At the same time, the fact that your late comers aren't participating in the *Value-Added Activities* will not interfere with their learning and complicate your teaching job.

Auditory Clarity

Practice speaking in front of a mirror and record what you are saying. Continue to do this until you notice that your mouth is opening fully and appropriately (compare yourself to newscasters and entertainers) and all your words are clear and easy to understand.

Voice Variations

Listen to professionals on the radio and television. As they are talking, they vary their voices in order to create interest and reduce boredom. Record yourself practicing varying your voice until you sound like a

radio or television personality that would be
respected by an audience or students like yours.

Notes

Part Nine

Survival Techniques

Notes

Alpha Instructors Convey Confidence and Competence

Alpha Instructors convey confidence and competence whether or not they feel them. If you don't, your students will begin taking control of the classroom setting. They'll potentially heckle, ask irrelevant questions, disengage, attack, belittle, and may even take over the learning agenda.

Avoid Offending Others - Nineteen Critical Rules

1. Never use offensive language.
2. Never make gender, racial, religious, age, or ethnic slurs.
3. Never be sarcastic or condone sarcasm.
4. Never make sexual innuendos.
5. Never relate stories or jokes that may be considered inappropriate by any of your students.
6. Never talk about how much money you make or don't make.
7. Never say anything that could be interpreted as critical of students or anyone or any group they may value.
8. Never state how difficult your job is or appear condescending toward your students' jobs or responsibilities.
9. Never even suggest that your students are not engaging, motivated, caring, or respectful.
10. Never not walk-your-talk.
11. Never teach something you don't totally understand and value.
12. Never fail to anticipate and respond to the needs and wishes of your students.
13. Never think your students shouldn't complain about something.
14. Never not address your students' needs.
15. Never appear dominating, controlling, arrogant, egotistical, or self-centered.
16. Never appear like a wimp.
17. Never fail to apologize when appropriate.
18. Never say or do things that are problem issues, words, or topics for your students.
19. Never fail to take responsibility for your teaching and either overtly or covertly blame your students or anyone else your students their lack of success.

Notes

Notes

Use Success Secrets of Others - Eighteen Ways to Increase Teaching Success

1. Frame what you are teaching positively from your students' perceived needs, desires, and perspectives.
2. Teach based on your students' past, positive experiences and memories.
3. Always be honest and do what you say you're going to do.
4. Use language acceptable to your grandmother and local religious leaders.
5. Avoid anything that could be construed as a slur toward anyone or any group.
6. Eliminate sarcasm and put-downs.
7. Speak without sexual innuendos or relate stories or jokes that any group may consider inappropriate.
8. Build trust by being vulnerable – expose truths about yourself.
9. Show true respect for your students, their lives, and their accomplishments.
10. Build a focus around a shared problem or adversary.
11. When doing anything that surfaces emotions, which can be an excellent strategy, provide for recovery and redirecting.
12. Always walk-your-talk.
13. Teach only what you totally understand and value.
14. Anticipate and respond to the needs and wishes of your students – if your students believe they need it, or if they want it badly enough, take care of it or be willing to lose those students.
15. Ensure others see you as caring, respectful, humble, sincere, confident, competent, and collaborative.
16. Apologize when something is not right. Thank students for their understanding, and move on.
17. Take responsibility for your students' success.
18. Ask, don't tell.

When Something is Going Wrong

Whatever is not right, pause and take several good deep breaths. Give yourself time and oxygen to regroup. Remember, your students have had trouble before, so take a moment, get the air you need, and figure out a good next step, which often includes:

■ Apologizing for whatever is not right.

- Asking who has been in a similar situation before and forgotten something, had an equipment failure, or whatever – then laughing about it.
- Thanking your students for their understanding.
- Starting where you left off or making a shift to a next point.

The Obnoxious Student Who States an Offensive Position

Remain calm, pause, make eye contact, and take at least one deep breath with your mouth slightly open. If it is true and appropriate, say to the entire group, "I know of many people who have that same opinion or belief. Raise your hand if you know of others with a similar perspective. Thank you. I recognize people's right to their opinion, but I don't share that opinion in this case.

When Someone Goes After You

- Take a deep breath with your mouth open and listen for what the real issues are.
- Assess quickly by looking how the rest of your students are responding.
- Try to listen and protect your adversary's dignity, don't validate anything you disagree with, but recognize people's rights to opinions.

- Avoid battles and look for a way to get together later to really talk it out.
- Consider asking them what they need or want to correct the situation, and offer what you can.
- Ask before going on if your adversary is at least OK with the settlement or the agreement for next steps.
- Do something that is energizing and that promotes positive feeling from the rest of your students. To get things moving again, consider a funny, distracting, story that is not belittling of anything or anyone.

Reducing Distracting Questions

Keep everything fast-paced and convey through your speed, stories, and content that you are an expert. If questions that are irrelevant surface, protect the dignity of the questioner, but share that their question addresses something outside your expertise or power to address. Request permission to, or simply state that you will stay focused on the topic at hand to make sure that time is efficiently used.

Notes

Notes

Resources

Notes

Resources

- Allen, Rich Ph.D. *Train Smart: Perfect Trainings Every Time.* The Brain Store
- Allen, Richard Howell. *Impact Teaching.* Allyn and Bacon
- Burmark, Lynell. *Visual Literacy: Learn to See, See to Learn.* ASCD
- Csikszentmihalyi, Mihaly. *Flow – The Psychology of Optimal Experience.* Harper Perennial
- Glasser, William. *Choice Theory.* Harper Collins
- Goleman, Daniel. *Emotional Intelligence.* Bantam
- Hyerle, David. *Visual Tools for Constructing Knowledge.* ASCD
- Jensen, Eric. *Super Teaching.* The Brain Store
- Jensen, Eric. *Brain-Based Learning.* The Brain Store
- Jensen, Eric. *Teaching with the Brain in Mind.* ASCD
- Mamchur, Carolyn. *Cognitive Type Theory & Learning Style.* ASCD
- Marzano, Robert, Pickering, Debra, Pollock, Jane. *Classroom Instruction that Works.* ASCD/MCREL
- McCombs, Barbara L. and James E. Pope. *Motivating Hard to Reach Students.* APA
- Oakley, Ed and Doug Krug. *Enlightened Leadership.* Simon & Schuster
- Sousa, David. How the Brain Learns & Learning Manual. Corwin & NASSP
- Wlodkowski, Raymond J. *Enhancing Adult Motivation to Learn.* Jossey-Bass
- Wlodkowski, Raymond J. and Margery B. Ginsberg. *Diversity and Motivation.* Jossey-Bass
- Wolfe, Patricia. *Brain Matters: Translating Research into Classroom Practice.* ASCD
- Wong, Harry and Rosemary Tripi. *First Days of School.* Harry K. Wong Publication

PEAK Publications

The High Performance Toolbox: Succeeding with Performance Tasks, Projects, and Assessments, 3rd Edition, by Spence Rogers, Shari Graham, and the Peak Learning Systems' Team.

Motivation & Learning: A Teacher's Guide to Building Excitement for Learning and Igniting the Drive for Quality by Spence Rogers, Jim Ludington, & Shari Graham.

Teaching Tips: 105 Ways to Increase Motivation & Learning, by Spence Rogers, and the Peak Learning Systems' Team.

Teaching Treasures: 229 Prompts to Make Learning by All a Dream Come True by Spence Rogers, and the Peak Learning Systems' Team.

Teaching and Training Techniques: Lighting the Way to Performance Excellence by Spence Rogers, Becky Graf, and Jim Ludington

Teaching for Execellence by Spence Rogers, Becky Graf, and Jim Ludington

PEAK Websites

www.peaklearn.com

www.new-teacher.com

Notes

Notes

Index

Notes

Index

Notes

Notes

_____
_____
_____
_____
_____
_____
_____
_____
_____
_____
_____
_____
_____
_____
_____
_____
_____
_____
_____
_____
_____
_____
_____

Notes

Notes

Notes

Notes

Index

Notes

_____

Notes

Notes

Notes